A Place Prepared

Insights into Revelation, Book 4

Other Books by the Author

The Coming End of the Age

An Overview of the Endtime

Preparing For the Lord's Return

Greapa

The Coming of the King in Matthew 24 and 25

The Goal and Peak of Our Christian Experience
Insights into Revelation, Book 1

The Beast, His Image, and His Mark
Insights into Revelation, Book 2

Firstfruits and Harvest
Insights into Revelation, Book 3

The Church in Philadelphia
Insights into Revelation, Book 5

Delusion and God's Salvation

A Faithful God

Booklets by the Author

The Heart of God	The Rapture
The Heart of God II	Urgency or Complacency
The Heart of God III	A New Creation
The Heart of God IV	The Spirit
The Heart of God V	The Spirit Was Not Yet
The Heart of God VI	The Lark Ascending
Redemption and Salvation	The Order of Melchizedek
Signs of the End	The Prayer of the End

Visit **aplaceinthewilderness.com** for more about these books (including their introduction, table of contents, and ordering information) and booklets.

A Place Prepared

Insights into Revelation, Book 4

Paul Cozza

A Place in the Wilderness

A Place Prepared
Insights into Revelation, Book 4

© 2019 Paul Cozza

ISBN 978-1-5136-4036-5

All rights reserved.
No part of this publication may be reproduced or transmitted in any form or by any means – electronic, mechanical, or any other, including photocopy, recording, or any information or retrieval system – without prior written consent, in hardcopy paper form, from:

Paul Cozza
A Place in the Wilderness

Website: aplaceinthewilderness.com
Email: paul@aplaceinthewilderness.com

Second printing: July, 2025

Scripture quotations are from the American Standard Version of the Bible (1901) unless otherwise noted.

Background world topological map courtesy NASA

Cover design: Nuggitz Creative Services (Nuggitz.com)
Cover photo: © 2016 znm666 | DepositPhotos.com

Table of Contents

Preface 1
Introduction 3
   The Central Theme 4
   An Overview 5
Chapter 1 – The Woman 7
   In Travail 8
   Worldwide Persecution 9
Chapter 2 – The Wilderness 11
   God's Judgments 11
   The Sixth Seal 12
   The Seventh Seal 13
   The First Trumpet 14
   The Second Trumpet 15
   The Third Trumpet 16
   The Fourth Trumpet 16
   Indirect Effects 17
   An Earth in Upheaval 18
   The Result 18
   The Great Eagle 20
   Apart 21
Chapter 3 – Flight and Refuge 31
   Slaughter 32
   The Third 33
   The Place 34
   Preparation 35
   Nourished 36
   A Warning 37
   Return 38

Chapter 4 – Hope **41**
   The Condition of the Believers *42*
   Unknowing *42*
   Growth *43*
   Repentance *44*
   Encouragement *44*
   The Wedding Feast *45*
   Adam and Eve *45*
   Pursue *47*

Chapter 5 – A Final Word **49**
   Move and Countermove *49*
   Satan Versus God *50*
   Clarity *50*
   Looking to the End *51*
   What Must We Do? *51*
   God's People *52*
   Great Need *53*
   Led by the Lord *53*

Bibliography **55**

Note to the reader
Explanations and further details about the text appear as footnotes. Scripture references are cited in the numbered **References** list at the end of each chapter.

Preface

I retired in 1991, hoping to spend the rest of my life in service to the Lord. As it turned out, He had something better in store for me. However, at that time I saw the matter of the wilderness in Revelation 12.[1] I had a heart to help in some way with the preparation of the place in the wilderness[2] where the majority of believers will be spiritually fed during the last three and a half years of this age. As the time of the end approaches, I've felt to write something about this wilderness and the place for God's people, but have been waiting for the right time to pen a short book.

Given the rise of evil in this country and worldwide, I believe now is that time. Consider the slaughter of the innocents, the unborn children, taking place in the United States. This evil was dictated by godless judges, judges with seared consciences, all in the name of a fabricated choice, that of a woman over her own body. No thought was given to the unborn child within the woman who could not voice his or her choice to live. How despicable the action of such judges is.

Consider the gross immorality, perversion, and abomination taking place in this country at this time. Unspeakable things are not only being openly practiced, but triumphantly displayed and even celebrated. Clearly, as Paul prophesied, the restraining One has been taken out of the way[3] and lawlessness with its accompanying evil is now rampaging throughout the United States and the whole world.

However, the blatant evil seen in the nefarious, sneaky, subtle, and dark actions of certain evil politicians in the recent confirmation of a Supreme Court justice of the United States, actions which put on display allegations that were not only uncorroborated but in every case contradicted, made clear to me that now is the time to write about what is really going on in this country. It is not a matter of left versus right, or liberal versus conservative. Something much more profound is occurring in the United States.

Hopefully this book will shed some light on what is really happening behind the scenes in the spiritual realm. Satan's plot needs to be exposed and brought into the light that we, God's children, might see, understand, and act appropriately. Seeing these things, we Christians must fight the spiritual battle to push back the darkness and allow God the freedom to move on the earth for the accomplishment of His purpose. May we all be strengthened inwardly into the inner man[4] to stand for God's desire and purpose.

References

[1] Rev. 12:6
[2] Rev. 12:6, 14
[3] 2 Thes. 2:7
[4] Eph. 3:16

Introduction

Revelation is a book of mysteries and hidden treasures, so many that they seem to be innumerable. Book after book could be written about the mysteries in Revelation, and in fact, the more we see there, the more there is to see.

Revelation is like some unimaginable, multi-dimensional puzzle, which appears impossible to piece together. To unlock this book requires divine resolve. To find and apprehend the hugely important nuances woven into the fabric of this book requires prayer, prayer, and more prayer. We must be like that woman of whom the Lord spoke[1] who came to a judge ceaselessly, asking him to avenge her of her adversary. We must come to the Lord relentlessly to open this book and get into its depths. We must come back to this book again and again, praying, asking, digging, knocking, and even demanding from the Lord the riches God has buried in it.

As we do this, slowly interlocking pieces are found. If pieces don't seem to quite fit, if there is the sensation that our understanding is not quite right, then something is missing. There must be something more, or perhaps something is out of place that we don't yet see. Our spirit knows when the puzzle picture is true. If we have a sense of inaccuracy, it is an indication to continue to seek and pray, to bother the Lord until He gives a full and open view of this book.

To grasp Revelation we must spend much time in prayer and communion with God. Through such an exercise, repeated over many years, the book of Revelation will open up. Not only so, and more importantly, through such a practice we are changed. Our concepts and even our way of thinking are transformed[2] by the constant contact with God's Word and with the Spirit of God embodied in His Word.[3] This continual communion with God Himself slowly changes us in our mind, emotion, and will. Our perceptions change from earthly to heavenly. We begin to perceive as God perceives. We are forced to reconsider our understanding of Revelation and God's Word generally. This leads us into new conceptual avenues, ways we had not previously imagined. Through this our minds are renewed and we are transformed. Eventually, like the apostle Paul,[4] we will be able to say that we have the mind of Christ.

This kind of practice requires us to appropriate and exercise the divine patience, persistence, and strength. How many Christian students of the Bible give up their study of Revelation before reaching its depths, mysteries, and hidden riches? How many merely accept sugar-coated doctrines, rather than the buried treasures in Revelation? How many stop chewing the tough "jerky" of this book — spitting it out — before extracting the nourishment within it? Yet, it is full of light, nourishment, encouragement, warning, and admonition. Truly, as the Word says, Blessed are those who keep the words of this book for the time is at hand![5]

The Central Theme

In the first book[*] of this series we saw the goal and peak of our Christian experience — the high mountain of the eternal state in Christ before our Father God in love. There is nothing to compare with this experience and it is for this that God has created us, saved us, and called us.

In the second book we traveled from the high mountaintop of God our Father to the depths of hell where we saw the beast — the Antichrist, his image in the temple in Jerusalem, and his mark upon the foreheads of his followers. While God brings His believers to the highest possible state of being, Satan deceives his followers into the lowest, most vile and foul condition.

The third book compared the two reapings of the believers at the end of this age — the firstfruits and the harvest. There we saw how the maturity, time, place, means, and state of being of these two greatly differ.

In these books much time has been spent encouraging the believers to run towards the goal of the high mountain peak that has been set before us. The prize of the firstfruits has been on display in order that we, the believers, might be drawn toward it. God is calling us to come forward to that for which we have been

---

[*] *The Goal and Peak of Our Christian Experience*

predestined,[6] to come forward *in this age* before the Lord returns, to run after Christ,[7] gain Christ,[8] and attain the goal.[9]

However, what of those Christian who don't come forward, who don't gain Christ, who are not sufficiently mature as the end of the age approaches? This book focuses on these, the majority of Christians, who will not be taken before the great tribulation. It centers on Revelation 12 where the universal woman — that great sign — is seen fleeing to her place in the wilderness.

In isolation, this portion of Revelation 12 seems impossible to understand. Some have made the mistake of thinking that the woman refers to Mary, the mother of Jesus, and the manchild to Jesus Himself. We can dismiss this error, however, by simply noting that there is no record of the mother of Jesus fleeing into the wilderness for three and a half years after the Lord's ascension. Others have concluded that the woman refers to Israel. However, such an understanding also does not align with what is presented in Revelation 12.

In order to understand this portion we must read it in conjunction with other parts of Revelation and the Bible. When we do, a picture begins to form. When we then take into account the present-day situation on earth, the woman and the wilderness come into focus. In this book I hope to convey what the Lord has shown concerning this and the scene before my eyes regarding God's people and their place in the endtime wilderness.

An Overview

In Chapter 1 we look at the woman: who she is, and when and where the events concerning her in Revelation 12 take place. This has been covered in previous books of this series, but it is necessary to repeat it here. Without a proper understanding of the woman, the rest of this book may not be understandable.

Chapter 2 concerns the wilderness and God's judgments at the beginning of the tribulation. These also have been covered before, but they are detailed here in a particular way: the relationship between God's judgments and the wilderness is described. The severity of God's judgments is beyond our capacity to imagine. Not many students of endtime prophecy realize that the world — the entire satanic system of things on the earth — will end.

It will be destroyed, and most of that destruction will occur at the beginning of the great tribulation. Given that, how can there be a place for the woman in the wilderness?

In Chapter 3 we look at the woman's flight into a refuge in the wilderness. The woman is fleeing, but from where? And, why is she fleeing? The woman flees into the wilderness to the place prepared for her. Where is this place and how is it prepared? Who is nourishing the woman there, and why is the place called a wilderness?

Chapter 4 talks of hope. Whether one is taken before the great tribulation or left to pass through the suffering of the last three and a half years, there is hope. Even if one is in the wilderness, there is hope! There is a blessing to be had! Chapter 4 describes this blessing.

Chapter 5 gives a final word. If we grasp the first four chapters of this book, we will see that there is a need for every goodhearted Christian to prepare for those times. We need to prepare for both ourselves and for others.

In addition, after reading this book hopefully many will see today's United States with different eyes and be strengthed to fight the spiritual battle for the Lord's interest on the earth. This final word delves into these matters.

May the Lord bless you in your reading!

References

[1] Luke 18:1-8
[2] Rom. 12:2
[3] Eph. 6:17
[4] 1 Cor. 2:16
[5] Rev. 1:3
[6] Eph. 1:3-6
[7] Song 1:4
[8] Phil. 3:7-8
[9] Phil. 3:10

CHAPTER 1

The Woman

And a great sign was seen in heaven: a woman arrayed with the sun, and the moon under her feet, and upon her head a crown of twelve stars... (Rev. 12:1)

The universal woman in Revelation 12 signifies the totality of God's people.* That is, she includes all of God's people from the time of the patriarchs to the Lord's second coming. She embraces both Christians and Jews, New Testament believers and Old Testament saints.

The patriarchs — the people of God before the giving of the law — are signified by the crown of twelve stars on her head; Israel of the Old Testament is signified by the moon upon which she stands; the church is shown by the sun in which she is clothed. She is comprised of all of God's redeemed.

Recall Jacob's dream. There, God's people on the earth were signified by the sun, the moon, and twelve stars. Similarly, in Revelation twelve the woman clothed with the sun, moon, and twelve stars signifies God's people, particularly those on the earth during the endtime.

---

*As mentioned above, there are various interpretations of this woman. Some have conjectured that the woman with the manchild depicts Mary with Jesus. However, the fact that the woman flees into the wilderness to be nourished (Rev. 12:6) for 1260 days — the last three and a half years of this age — makes such an understanding untenable. Others have thought that the woman signifies Israel. However, Israel does not flee to escape persecution at the end of this age. Rather, she is the focus of the great tribulation (Matt. 24:21). In addition, the manchild "born" of the woman is comprised of Christians (Rev. 12:10). Therefore, Israel cannot be the woman. Finally, some have supposed this woman refers to the Church. This also cannot be the case, for the rest of her seed keep the commandments of God (Rev. 12:17). In the New Testament, Christ is the end of the law to those who believe (Rom. 10:4). Therefore, the seed spoken of here cannot be New Testament Christians. They must be Jews, specifically the 144,000 sealed in Revelation 7:3-8.

In Travail

...she crieth out, travailing in birth, and in pain to be delivered. (Rev. 12:2)

The woman is in travail to give birth, and in pain to be delivered. Literally in Greek, she *is being tormented* to be delivered. This is similar to the Lord's words in John.[1] It indicates that God's people are being persecuted and martyred. At the end of this age, many Christians will be slaughtered in a great, satanically-inspired mass murder of Christians. This persecution will stretch from Europe throughout Asia. It will be Satan's attempt to exterminate Christians from the earth, Christ from the world, and God from His creation. While this violence against God's people will arise chiefly in Europe and Asia, it will be widespread throughout the earth, occurring even in the United States. We can see the beginning of this already in the hatred of the far left toward Christians today.

As the end of this age approaches, this persecution will greatly intensify. By the time of the last three and a half years — commonly called the great tribulation — the persecution will reach its peak. Many will flee from the areas of greatest suffering — Europe and Asia — to a safe haven, which God is preparing and will prepare for His people. There, Christians will be fed both spiritually and physically during the last years before the Lord returns.

This persecution is already slowly starting. It will increase until the very end of the age, when it will force Christians to flee to the place prepared by God where they will be nourished during the great tribulation.

It is true that Christians have been persecuted from the time Christ walked on the earth until now. However, as the end of the age approaches this persecution and martyrdom will escalate greatly. It will be far more intense than at any time during the church age. Tens of thousands and perhaps even millions will be martyred. This slaughter of God's people will be so extreme that it will cause the martyrs resting under the earth* to cry out, as depicted in the opening of the fifth seal.²

During the endtime it will seem as if darkness has prevailed. Lawlessness will be unbounded, for the One who restrains³ will be taken out of the way, allowing Satan in his vile rebellion against God, hatred of the light, and violent murder of God's people to run rampant. We see this already to a small degree. It will get much worse as the end of the age nears and Satan sees his reign coming to an end. This is depicted in Revelation 12 and clearly mentioned in verse 12 of that chapter.

Worldwide Persecution

This persecution will be especially intense in Europe. Europe, North Africa, and part of the Middle East will be the Antichrist's Empire.⁴ He will not tolerate any religion.⁵ He will particularly hate⁶ Christ and Christians. Eventually, he will extirpate all Christians from his empire. Then it will be an empire of darkness, in darkness, and for darkness. The only light in his realm will be the two witnesses⁷ and the sealed of Israel.⁸ Eventually, even they will be killed or carried away into captivity.⁹

Asia, particularly China, will be the area where the persecution will probably be greatest. This is occurring now, and will intensify. It will likely spread throughout all of Asia. Only the Lord knows how many Christians will die under the persecuting hands of the Chinese communist authorities, the Russian bureaucracy, and the other governments in Asia.

This persecution will spread throughout the earth, to Africa and the Middle East as well as Asia and Europe. The Middle East is already a center of great anti-Christian hatred. Islam is a devilish anti-Christ movement with a sole purpose — to rid the earth of Christ and His people. By the time of the end, they will have succeeded in eliminating Christians from the Middle East. It is not

---

*The martyrs cry out from under the altar (Rev. 6:9-10). The "altar" on which they were offered is the earth where they were slain. Thus, they cry out from under the earth, from the pleasant section of Hades (Luke 23:43) where they are resting until their resurrection.

happenstance that at the sounding of the sixth trumpet two hundred million horsemen will march across Asia through the Middle East toward Israel, killing the third of men along the way. This is God's righteous judgment upon that concentrated evil in the Middle East.

Under such intense persecution the woman in Revelation 12 — God's people on the earth — will flee. The Christians will run from that persecution, seeking sanctuary and a place to recover and grow in Christ. But, to where will they go?

References

[1] Jn. 16:21
[2] Rev. 12:9-11
[3] 2 Thes. 2:7
[4] Dan. 8:9
[5] Dan. 11:37
[6] Dan. 11:36
[7] Rev. 11:3-13
[8] Rev. 7:4-8; 12:17
[9] Rev. 13:7, 10; 20:4

CHAPTER 2

The Wilderness

And the woman fled into the wilderness, where she hath a place prepared of God, that there they may nourish her a thousand two hundred and threescore days....And there were given to the woman the two wings of the great eagle, that she might fly into the wilderness unto her place, where she is nourished for a time, and times, and half a time, from the face of the serpent. (Rev. 12:6, 14)

The woman will flee into the wilderness to her place. The Greek word translated "wilderness" means a place apart from civilization. In our parlance, this is a place apart from the world, apart from the satanic system of things on the earth. It refers to an uncultivated area, one isolated and lonely.

Where on the earth today is there such a place? And, where is there a wilderness that could support so many of God's people, who are fleeing persecution? There will certainly be tens and hundreds of thousands of Christians fleeing the satanic genocide taking place in Europe, Asia, and elsewhere on the earth. Those escaping persecution may very well number in the millions. What wilderness on the earth today could support such an influx?

Furthermore, what area on the earth could be considered a wilderness, given the current state of technology and particularly communications, which are available virtually everywhere? In fact, there is apparently nowhere on earth that could meet the criteria of a wilderness able to support a huge inflow of God's people. However, what we see today will greatly change by the endtime.

God's Judgments

...they say to the mountains and to the rocks, Fall on us, and hide us from the face of him that sitteth on the throne, and from the

wrath of the Lamb: for the great day of their wrath is come; and who is able to stand? (Rev. 6:16-17)

The woman will flee into the wilderness, where she will be nourished for 1260 days — or times, time, and half a time. This will be the last three and a half years of this age, which is often called the great tribulation. However, at the beginning of those last three and a half years, God's judgments of the sixth and seventh seals and the first four trumpets take place. These judgments will drastically alter not only the world, but the earth itself. Much of the world will be destroyed, and most of the remainder will be heavily damaged. As we will see, what is considered civilized today will be changed into a wilderness. Roads, streets, highways, and superhighways will be empty, unused. Vast areas will be uninhabited. Generally speaking, the world as we know it will cease to exist.

Let us consider God's judgments of the sixth and seventh seals and the first four trumpets. All of these involve fire from the heavens. It is important to realize that these events are all aspects of one greater, all-encompassing event — a storm of asteroids* and meteoroids. This happening will take the earth by surprise.[1] Nearly the whole world will be totally unprepared.†

The Sixth Seal

And I saw when he opened the sixth seal, and there was a great earthquake; and the sun became black as sackcloth of hair, and

---

*It is evident that it is not a comet or fragments of a comet that will strike the earth during the endtime. Comets are easily visible as they near the sun. Therefore, since the world is unaware of these judgments until they occur, what strikes the earth at that time must be asteroids and fragments of asteroids, not a comet.

†Scientists and astronomers are carefully watching the heavens for asteroids and comets that might damage the earth. But, their search is limited to areas near the solar system's ecliptic (the plane in the sky that the sun traces out during the year), because most asteroids and comets are found in that region of the sky. Since God's judgments at the beginning of the tribulation take the world by surprise, this storm of heavenly fire should appear from outside the area being searched by scientists — that is, from outside the ecliptic. When it happens it will be completely unexpected.

the whole moon became as blood; and the stars of the heaven fell unto the earth, as a fig tree casteth her unripe figs when she is shaken of a great wind. And the heaven was removed as a scroll when it is rolled up; and every mountain and island were moved out of their places. And the kings of the earth, and the princes, and the chief captains, and the rich, and the strong, and every bondman and freeman, hid themselves in the caves and in the rocks of the mountains... (Rev. 6:12-15)

When Christ opens the sixth seal, the whole Earth will be shaken. There will be an enormous earthquake and the stars will fall from the sky like figs being shaken from a fig tree by a great wind. Every mountain and island will be moved out of their places. Undoubtably, this will be an enormous meteor shower striking the earth. How much damage this will cause is not known, but it certainly won't be minor. Yet this is simply a warning to mankind concerning what is about to occur. It is the harbinger of the events to follow. If this momentous event that moves mountains and islands is simply a warning, consider how enormous and dire the ensuing judgments will be.

According to Joel,[2] which describes this same event from the perspective of Israel rather than from the earth generally, there will also be great pillars of smoke, which will be caused by the asteroid or meteoroid strikes mentioned in Revelation 6. This smoke will blot out the sun, darken much of the sky, and turn the moon blood red.

The Seventh Seal

And when he opened the seventh seal, there followed a silence in heaven about the space of half an hour. And I saw the seven angels that stand before God; and there were given unto them seven trumpets. And another angel came and stood over the altar, having a golden censer; and there was given unto him much incense, that he should add it unto the prayers of all the saints upon the golden altar which was before the throne. And the smoke of the incense, with the prayers of the saints, went up before God out of the angel's hand. And the angel taketh the censer; and he filled it with the fire of the altar, and cast it upon the earth: and there followed thunders, and voices, and lightnings, and an earthquake. (Rev. 8:1-5)

When Christ opens the seventh seal, there is silence in heaven for half an hour. This indicates the solemnity of what is about to happen. Christ will then cast fire upon the earth, and so the destruction of the world and the judgment of mankind will commence. Those who have trusted in the world, enjoyed the world, loved the world, and been corrupted by the world will suffer God's judgment along with the world. God will destroy the world and all that is in it. Those who have attached themselves to the world will suffer destruction along with it.

The First Trumpet

And the first sounded, and there followed hail and fire, mingled with blood, and they were cast upon the earth: and the third part of the earth was burnt up, and the third part of the trees was burnt up, and all green grass was burnt up. (Rev. 8:7)

At the sounding of the first trumpet fire and hail will pummel the earth. A huge storm of meteoroids will enter the Earth's atmosphere and superheat from friction as they traverse it. The enormous heat generated by the huge number of fiery meteoroids in the atmosphere will cause massive damage on earth. Many of these meteoroids will strike the earth. The third of the trees and land will be burned, along with all the green grass across the face of the earth.

As we have seen in previous books,* the third that will be burned does not refer to a general third of the earth, but rather to that particular most evil third — the Asian mainland.† That continent will suffer immense destruction from this judgment. In addition, all the earth will be damaged to a lesser degree.

That the first trumpet mainly affects Asia indicates that the persecution and slaughter of Christians during the endtime will

---

*See *The Coming End of the Age* and *Preparing for the Lord's Return* for a detailed explanation of God's endtime judgments.

†Only Asia could account for a third of the earth's land mass. The other continents are too small.

occur to the greatest degree in Asia. As a result of the Christian genocide carried out by the Asian governments, God will respond with this severe judgment. His righteous judgment upon Asia is His reply to the cry of the martyred saints at the opening of the fifth seal. The extent of the damage from the first trumpet is depicted in Map 1 at the end of this chapter.

The Second Trumpet

And the second angel sounded, and as it were a great mountain burning with fire was cast into the sea: and the third part of the sea became blood; and there died the third part of the creatures which were in the sea, even they that had life; and the third part of the ships was destroyed. (Rev. 8:8-9)

When the second trumpet sounds, a great burning mountain strikes the sea — that is, a huge asteroid, measuring miles across, will impact the Pacific Ocean.* The damage done by this will be immeasurable. The heat generated by the asteroid's passage through the atmosphere, the concussive force of the impact, and the tsunamis striking the Pacific coastland will kill hundreds of millions. As we will see below, the indirect deaths caused by this asteroid strike might exceed that.

That this asteroid will strike the Pacific, obliterating the entire Pacific rim, indicates that this area is the most evil part of the earth. Consequently, it will suffer this most grave judgment from God. Even today we can see the evil fermenting there. This malevolence will intensify greatly as the end nears.

We simply cannot conceive of the destruction that will be caused by this enormous asteroid. Our minds recoil at the thought of what will happen not only around the Pacific Rim but also worldwide when this asteroid impacts the earth. The damage from the heat, concussive forces, tsunamis, earthquakes, and volcanic eruptions due to this asteroid strike is simply unimaginable.

The areas of immediate destruction caused by this impactor are shown in Map 2.

---

*It is only in the Pacific that a third of the sea could be affected as detailed in this judgment. None of the other oceans are large enough.

The Third Trumpet

And the third angel sounded, and there fell from heaven a great star, burning as a torch, and it fell upon the third part of the rivers, and upon the fountains of the waters; and the name of the star is called Wormwood: and the third part of the waters became wormwood; and many men died of the waters, because they were made bitter. (Rev. 8:10-11)

When the third trumpet sounds a great star will fall upon the third part of the rivers and the fountains of waters. This will be another asteroid strike. It will not be as large and destructive as that of the second trumpet, but will nevertheless cause an enormous amount of damage. This asteroid will fall upon the Himalayas,* melting the snow cap and in some way poisoning the waters that flow out to all of Asia. Many men will die because of these poisoned waters.

The poisoning of these waters will most likely be due to the toxins, such as sulphuric acid, that will be formed by the fiery cataclysm of this asteroid impact. A number of such toxins could be produced in the air by such an event, and foul the waters as they settle to earth.

The approximate area damaged by this asteroid is shown in Map 3.

The Fourth Trumpet

And the fourth angel sounded, and the third part of the sun was smitten, and the third part of the moon, and the third part of the stars; that the third part of them should be darkened, and the day should not shine for the third part of it, and the night in like manner. (Rev. 8:12)

The fourth trumpet is the aftermath of the seventh seal and first three trumpets. Due to the enormous amount of debris ejected into the atmosphere by the previous asteroid and meteoroid impacts, one-third of the earth will be darkened. Over one-third of

---

*Where else could a third part of the rivers and fountains of waters be poisoned by a single asteroid strike? Furthermore, this will be yet another judgment upon that particular, most evil third of the earth — Asia.

the earth there will be a thick cloud of ejecta darkening the sun, moon, stars, and sky generally.

This will mainly affect Asia, but will also be problematic for the more northern latitudes. Temperatures will drop precipitously,* particularly in those areas where sunlight is greatly diminished. Most crops and plants will die. The northern latitudes will become uninhabitable due to the lack of sunlight and plummeting temperatures.

How many will die from starvation or exposure we do not know, but it must be a great number — this trumpet is one of God's judgments. Many will attempt an arduous southward journey without mechanized vehicles of any kind, in an attempt to escape a slow death in the frozen wasteland of the north. Of these, many will perish en route. The environment at that time will be most miserable, chaotic, and inhospitable.

Map 4 shows the areas that should be most affected by this change in climate.

Indirect Effects

In addition to the devastation directly caused by this enormous storm from the heavens, there will be a massive amount of indirect damage. The antipode† of the strike of the great asteroid of the second trumpet (and to a lesser degree the asteroid strike of the third trumpet) will experience enormous upheaval as the energy from this asteroid impact passes through the earth and reaches the opposite side. The coastal and lowland areas of south and west Africa, most of South America, and the west coast of Australia will be in great peril. Tsunamis will be generated at the antipode by the transmitted concussive force from the impact, and travel throughout the Atlantic Ocean and perhaps the Indian Ocean (as well as the south Pacific for the strike of the third trumpet).

---

*It has been estimated that temperatures dropped about 45° Fahrenheit from the asteroid strike that caused the demise of the dinosaurs. The first three trumpets may cause a similar, drastic change of climate.

† The point on the earth's surface that is diametrically opposite.

Millions more will die as the tsunamis devastate the great cities along the imperiled coastlines and lay waste to huge swaths of inhabited land. There will be no escape from these upheavals. See Map 5 for those areas in jeopardy from these aftereffects.

An Earth in Upheaval

In addition, the violent shaking of the earth from these many impacts will result in earthquakes and volcanic eruptions throughout the globe, particularly along the earth's fault lines. Earthquake upon earthquake will rattle the earth. Many of these will be enormous. The earth will then shudder from tens of thousands and perhaps hundreds of thousands of aftershocks. No place will escape this shaking.

Furthermore, erupting volcanoes will spew immense amounts of ash into the air and outflow lava onto surrounding areas, as the earth's molten core is concussed, compressed, and forced to the surface.

Skyscrapers will be toppled, buildings leveled, and houses collapsed as one violent tremblor after another passes through the earth. Areas around volcanoes will be swallowed in lava or suffocated in ash. It will appear that no place on earth is safe.

Areas having a risk of earthquakes or volcanic activity are shown in Map 6.

The Result

After such a destructive onslaught, what will remain on the earth that has even a semblance of habitability? It would seem that nearly the entire Earth will be destroyed. Indeed, by overlaying the more serious effects shown in the previously cited maps of God's endtime judgments, we can determine to some degree what areas will suffer the least amount of devastation. This aggregation is depicted in Map 7.

The massive destruction caused by God's judgments at the beginning of the great tribulation will leave few areas on the earth in even a marginably habitable condition. As can be seen in the Map 7, most regions will not escape. In spite of all the worldwide destruction, southern Europe and the area around the Mediterranean, including Israel, will be in comparatively good condition. And, it must be so because the Antichrist's empire and Israel must remain for the fulfillment of prophecy.

A part of central and western Australia may survive that time intact. Similarly, parts of central Africa may also pass through those judgments without excessive damage. In addition, a small part of eastern South America may remain somewhat habitable.

The south central United States will also fair better then most areas on the earth. Parts of Kansas, Oklahoma, Texas, the southeast US, and certain other adjoining areas should escape that destruction with perhaps minimal damage.

Of these five areas that will suffer less extensive damage, which could support an influx of hundreds of thousands of Christians fleeing persecution as the tribulation approaches? As mentioned previously, there will be a great persecution at the end of the age. Many Christians will flee from that to a place prepared by God.[3] Then God's judgments will strike the earth. The Christians who have fled will have to be in a place that keeps them from harm at the time of God's judgments, and also provides a habitat that can support them for the last 1260 days of this age.

While the five previously mentioned areas might provide some protection during God's judgments, not all of them can provide the habitat and environment necessary to support such a huge number of Christians. Europe and the area around the Mediterranean cannot be this place. In fact, Christians will be fleeing the persecution in that area.

Central Africa cannot support its current population. How could it possibly support a great influx of refugees during the tribulation, at a time when the situation there will be much worse? Central Africa therefore cannot be the wilderness spoken of in Revelation 12.

Western-central Australia might provide some shelter, protection, and habitability. However, there would need to be great change before the endtime for this to occur. The area of Australia that will likely escape great destruction is currently largely uninhabited, inhospitable, unfarmed, and arid. Unless there is a drastic change to that area, it will not be able to sustain a large number of refugees during the endtime, when governmental support and services no longer exist. In addition, this area is susceptible to earthqueakes, especially in the extreme conditions that will exist during God's endtime judgments.

The area in South America that may escape severe destruction is generally in the higher elevations of eastern Brazil. The terrain there is mostly savannah, parts of which have been improved to grow crops. In some areas there is much poverty; in others the populace is more prosperous. This part of Brazil might be able to support some of the Christians that will flee persecution. However, Brazil's immigration policies are currently unequiped to handle large numbers of refugees. All things being considered, it is doubtful that the small area of Brazil that might escape damage at the beginning of the tribulation could support the great influx of immigrants that will be seeking refuge during the endtime.

That leaves the south-central United States. Much of the land from Kansas southward is quite desirable from a commercial perspective, being good for grazing or farming. During the endtime, once the climate on earth starts to return to some semblance of normalcy, this area could support a very large number of refugees. Furthermore, this is an area well known for its God-fearing people, those who love Christ and believe in the Bible. The proper and upstanding humanity in so many of the residents of this area is readily apparent to those who spend time there and look.

The Great Eagle

And there were given to the woman the two wings of the great eagle, that she might fly into the wilderness unto her place, where she is nourished for a time, and times, and half a time, from the face of the serpent. (Rev. 12:14)

In addition, in Revelation 12 we are told that the woman will be given the two wings of the great eagle to fly into the wilderness. While the great eagle might be only a reference to God Himself, it is also possible that God in His foresight, knowing what was about to come to pass, used the "great eagle" purposely to refer to the United States, whose emblem is the Bald Eagle.

For these reasons I believe that the place prepared by God in the wilderness for the woman during the last three and a half years of this age will be in the south-central United States. There the woman will be nourished and the believers will grow in Christ as they await the Lord's return.

Apart

The south-central United States today would not be considered a wilderness under any circumstances. However, God's judgments at the beginning of the great tribulation will change the whole earth. Across the globe, civilization as we know it will cease to exist nearly totally. The satanic world will be ended, except in the Antichrist's empire and regions surrounding it.

There will be no more electricity, communications, facilities, commerce, and the other aspects of the world that we take for granted today. There will be shortages of food, water, medical supplies, and every other necessity. After the great asteroid strikes, marking the beginning of the time of trial,[4] temperatures will plummet; it will be impossible to grow anything. Until the debris settles from the earth's atmosphere, living will be extraordinarily difficult.

That time will be like living in a terrifying nightmare.[5] But once the climate begins to revert, and temperatures warm so that the earth can sustain crops, the farmers and ranchers of the south-central United States will produce food for all that are there, with the help of the abundant manpower available from the great flood of refugees.

Today's world will be gone. That area will become a real wilderness, fully separated from today's civilization. But in that place, God's people will be nourished and sustained until the Lord returns. While it will be a wilderness, there God will care for His people.

Map 1 – The Devastation from the First Trumpet

The Wilderness 23

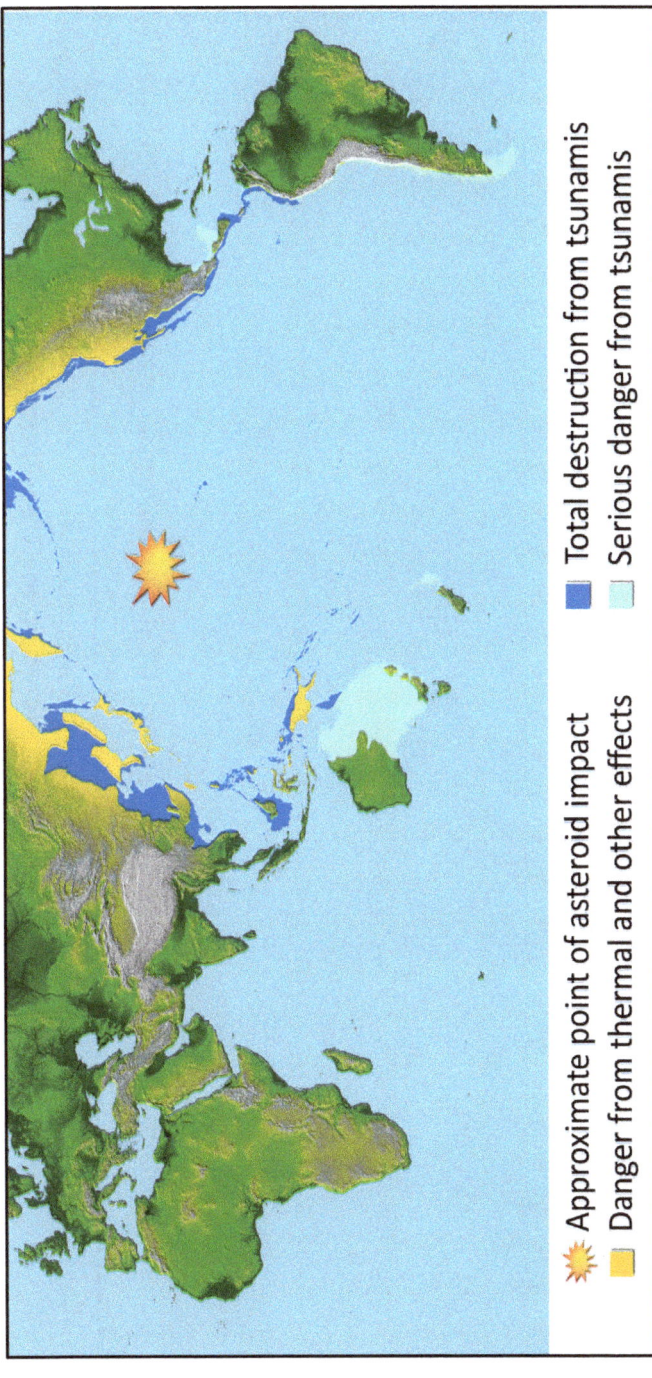

Map 2 – The Devastation from the Second Trumpet

Map 3 – The Devastation from the Third Trumpet

The Wilderness 25

Map 4 – The Darkness and Cold of the Fourth Trumpet

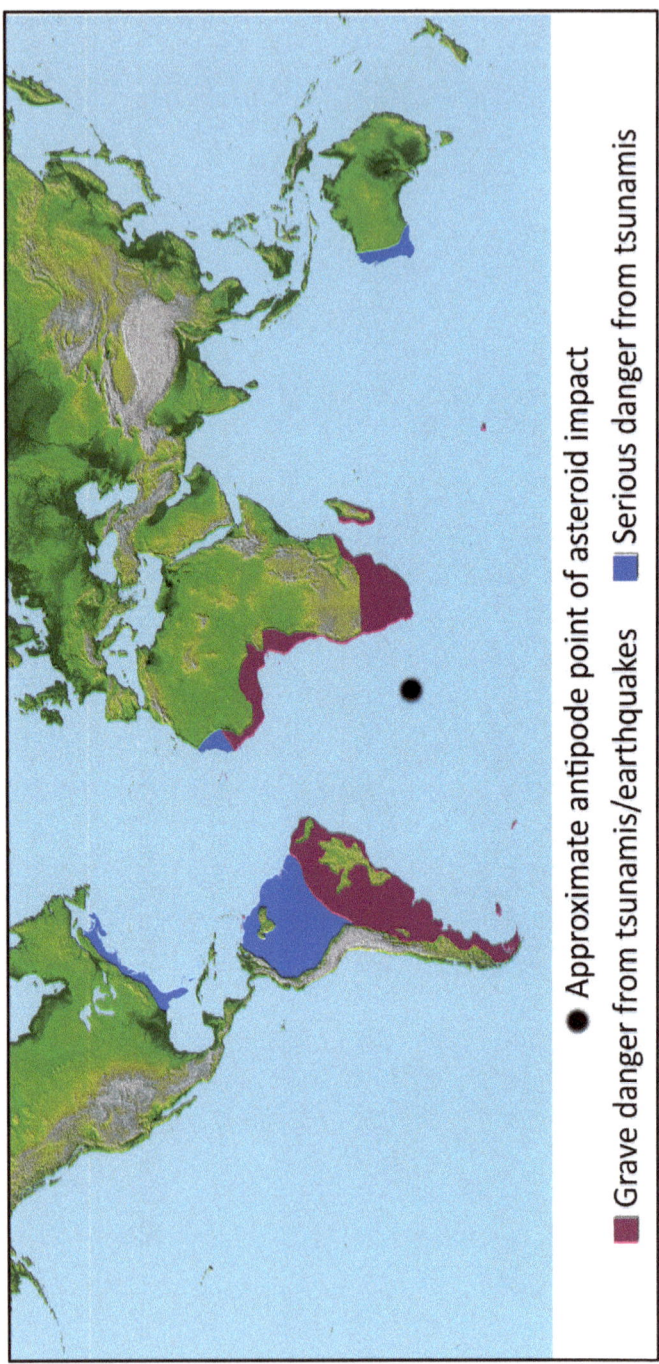

Map 5 – The Effects Around the Antipode of the Trumpet 2 Asteroid Impact

The Wilderness 27

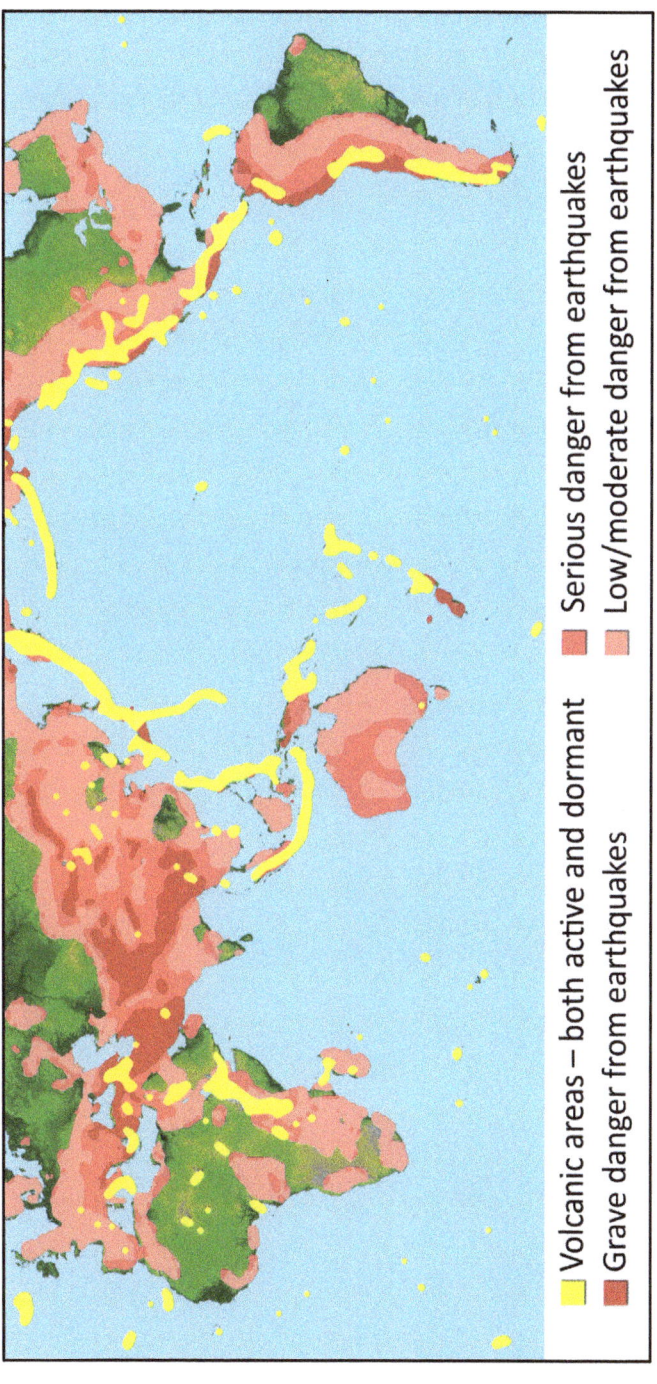

Map 6 – Areas at Risk from Earthquake and Volcanic Activity

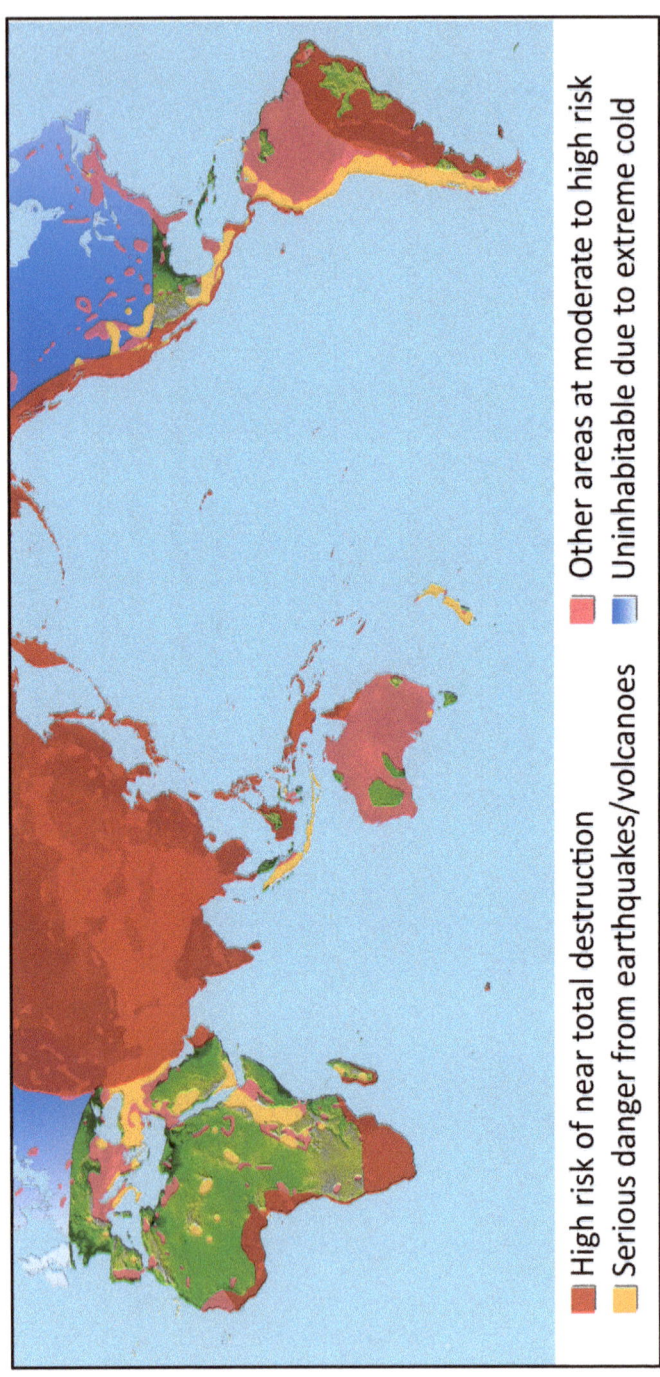

Map 7 – Destruction Caused by the Endtime Judgments

References

[1] Lk. 21:34-35
[2] Joel 2:30-31
[3] Rev. 12:6
[4] Rev. 3:10
[5] Lk. 21:26

CHAPTER 3

Flight and Refuge

...and she was with child; and she crieth out, travailing in birth, and in pain to be delivered. (Rev. 12:2)

And the woman fled into the wilderness, where she hath a place prepared of God, that there they may nourish her a thousand two hundred and threescore days. (Rev. 12:6)

And when the dragon saw that he was cast down to the earth, he persecuted the woman that brought forth the man child. (Rev. 12:13)

The woman flees into the wilderness to a place God has prepared for her. Why is she fleeing? According to the context of Revelation 12, she is fleeing persecution.

First, she is in travail to give birth. She is *being tormented* to be delivered. For her to be in travail, to be tormented, indicates that she is suffering persecution. In John 16 the Lord likens His death and the suffering of His disciples to a woman in travail.[1] His death at the hands of the Jewish religionists and the Roman government was due to their persecution of Him and those who follow Him. Similarly, for the woman to be in travail in Revelation 12 is for God's people to be suffering persecution.

In addition, Satan is seeking to devour the woman's manchild.[2] He devours by killing those stronger believers who comprise the manchild.[3] This too indicates persecution and martyrdom.

In Revelation, the Word tells us explicitly that Satan persecutes God's people after being cast from the heavens. It is also said that the woman will be kept from the face of the serpent.[4] This indicates persecution as well. When Satan is cast from the heavens to earth, he will have great wrath.[5] He will seek to kill all God's people, whether Christian or Jew. He will even send a "flood" after the woman.[6] This indicates that he will send an army to try to destroy God's people. However, God will not allow this and will intervene.[7]

Finally, we are told that Satan will go forth to make war with the rest of the woman's seed. This pictures his vicious and malicious attack on those Jews who will be sealed[8] and who will travel throughout Israel speaking the gospel of the kingdom.[9]

God's people will be suffering extreme persecution at the end of this age. This will be something more than the persecution Christians have suffered throughout the centuries. It will be something much greater, much more widespread, and much more intense. It will be a great persecution, the final persecution.

While the evil inflicted on the believers over the centuries has been enormous, what will transpire at the end of this age will dwarf that. It will be something the world has never seen before. Satan will be incensed beyond measure. He will have been cast from the heavens to the earth, no longer able to stand before God and accuse God's people. His sphere of influence will be greatly limited. And he will know that his time is very short — he will have only three and a half years before he is bound in the abyss.

Although Satan will struggle to change the outcome of events leading up to the endtime, he will see all of his efforts come to naught. In great frustration over the fruitlessness of his endeavors as he sees the endtime unfolding exactly as prophesied in God's Word, and knowing what his future is, in fury and great wrath he will attack God's people with measureless rage and without restraint as he attempts to destroy them and God's plan.

Slaughter

And when he opened the fifth seal, I saw underneath the altar the souls of them that had been slain for the word of God, and for the testimony which they held: and they cried with a great voice, saying, How long, O Master, the holy and true, dost thou not judge and avenge our blood on them that dwell on the earth? And there was given them to each one a white robe; and it was said unto them, that they should rest yet for a little time, until their fellow-servants also and their brethren, who should be killed even as they were, should have fulfilled their course. (Rev. 6:9-11)

How many hundreds of thousands will be killed during this time only the Lord knows. The martyrs may number in the millions. In Asia particularly, the extent of this genocide will be unfathomable. The Chinese government particularly will be devoted to the murder of Christians. The Asian mainland will be a kind of abattoir for believers. Indeed, wherever the arm of the Chinese government reaches at that time, there will be slaughter.

Those who are able will flee the carnage. Hundreds of thousands from the Far East will flee to wherever they can find refuge, especially to the United States. The believers will escape from Asia, as well as every spot in which the persecution of Christians arises. They will flee from the Antichrist's empire in particular. Indeed, God calls the believers to come out from there so that they will not partake of the plagues that will afflict it.[10]

The believers will seek shelter in the United States. However, parts of the US will not accept them. As we can already see today, in certain regions of the US, such as the west and northeast coasts, there are many who hate God, hate Christ, hate the Bible, hate Christians, and hate the truth. These are rapidly becoming God-hating areas. During the endtime these will reject the Christian immigrants. But in the US heartland, in the area commonly referred to as the Bible Belt, the fleeing Christians will be welcomed and offered refuge.

The US heartland is the breadbasket of the United States. Much of the land is fertile, excellent for growing crops. In addition, a good portion is used for grazing cattle, sheep, or other animals. Even though the Earth will be in an extremely chaotic condition during the last years of this age from the wounds of God's judgments, this area will still be able to provide the necessities for God's people.

The Third

And the first sounded, and there followed hail and fire, mingled with blood, and they were cast upon the earth: and the third part of the earth was burnt up, and the third part of the trees was burnt up, and all green grass was burnt up. And the second angel sounded, and as it were a great mountain burning with fire was cast into the sea: and the third part of the sea became blood; and there died the third part of the creatures which were in the sea, even they that had life; and the third part of the ships was destroyed. And the third angel sounded, and there fell from heaven a great star, burning as a torch, and it fell upon the third part of the rivers, and upon the fountains of the waters; and the name of the star is called Wormwood: and the third part of the waters became wormwood; and many men died of the waters, because they were made bitter. And the fourth angel sounded, and the third part of the sun was smitten, and the third part of the moon, and the third part of the stars; that the third part of them should be darkened, and the day should not shine for the third part of it, and the night in like manner. (Rev. 8:7-12)

When we view the whole endtime picture concerning both God's people and His judgments, it becomes apparent why God will judge the world and why His judgments will fall on that particular *third* of the earth. Why are Asia and the Pacific Rim judged so harshly by God? Because it will be there that much of the slaughter of God's people will occur, and it is from there that God's people will flee.

While God's people will flee from Europe as well, God will withhold His hand of judgment from that part of the earth temporarily in order to bring Israel to salvation. However, at the time of His return, Europe and all the remaining armies of the world will suffer the most severe judgment of all.[11]

The Place

And the woman fled into the wilderness, where she hath a place prepared of God, that there they may nourish her a thousand two hundred and threescore days. (Rev. 12:6)

To where will the woman flee? God is already preparing this place for the believers — the woman in Revelation 12 — to be nourished at the end of this age. This should be in the southern United States from Kansas, Oklahoma, and Texas eastward. However, this area will not be as it is today — it will be a wilderness.

Today's world with all of its conveniences, luxuries, and amusements will be gone. God's judgments of the sixth and seventh seals along with the first four trumpets will devastate the satanic world. By this divine intervention the believers will be separated from what is called civilization. For those last years on the earth they will be apart from all the worldly diversions, which distracted them from God.

Many Christians think all the believers will be raptured to be with the Lord before those days. This is a serious error. Unfortunately, for many the realization of this error will only occur when they find themselves on earth, struggling to survive, during the time of trial[12] at the end of the age. Even though God will provide the means to live during those years, it will be extraordinarily difficult, physically and perhaps even more, psychologically.

The whole satanic world will be destroyed and no longer present as a source of supply. There will be *no* electricity, *no* commerce, *no* business, *no* money, *no* sports, *no* music, *no* movies, *no* amusements of any kind. There will be *no* religion and *no* denominations. Concerning everything of the world in which the believers today indulge themselves, the operative adjective will be "No!" No, no, no! All these things will be at an end. All that we take for granted today will be gone. During the endtime the believers will be struggling simply to live.

Preparation

God has been preparing and will continue to prepare this place in the wildeness specifically for the believers. We can see this happening today in the Bible Belt in the United States. Many of those living in this area are quite religious. While religion itself is simply another part of Satan's world that keeps men apart from God and acts as a substitute for Christ, nevertheless the truths in the Bible are spoken and shared among the believers to some degree. This has resulted in many being born again and indwelt by Christ.

Through such an interaction with the divine Spirit, the humanity among these people is slowly being uplifted toward the divine standard. As a consequence, the Christians in this area are often giving people, having open hearts and open homes. Unfortunately the world — and in many cases the religious world — has distracted many of these dear Christian brothers and sisters from seeking Christ to the full and maturing in Him into that for which God has saved them.

Nourished

And the woman fled into the wilderness, where she hath a place prepared of God, that there they may nourish her a thousand two hundred and threescore days. (Rev. 12:6)

And there were given to the woman the two wings of the great eagle, that she might fly into the wilderness unto her place, where she is nourished for a time, and times, and half a time, from the face of the serpent. (Rev. 12:14)

Because of this, during those last years the woman will need to be nourished. This sustenance will certainly include the physical — after all, without such nourishment the believers will die. However, more importantly it will include the spiritual.

The reason many believers will be left behind to pass through this tribulation is that they have not matured in Christ. This maturation is a matter of growth in the spiritual and divine life. Each born again believer possesses the divine life by virtue of his birth of the Holy Spirit.[13] But, how much has that divine life grown?[14] How much have each of us matured spiritually? How much of Christ have we gained?[15] For those believers left behind during the tribulation the answer is, *"Not enough."* As a consequence, they will need to be nourished spiritually.

The believers will be suffering physically. Many will be sick; others will be injured. There will be shortages of food, water, and medical supplies. In a word, the "woman" will be ill. This will be a reflection of the true spiritual condition of the believers at that time. Spiritually, many will be sick, malnourished, and thirsting[16] for God. Therefore, that last three and a half years will be a time for the believers to become healthy in Christ toward God.

Some of these believers will have the spiritual food to feed others. Through this, the believers will slowly return to spiritual health and begin to grow properly in Christ. With the world gone there will be nothing to continually distract the believers from God.

As the believers are being nourished and growing in the divine life, they will also be "dried out."[17] Many believers have enjoyed the world, taken part in it, and become one with the worldly things. Thus they have become part of the world themselves. The worldly element has been imparted into them and become part of them. That element is something of Satan, something dark and evil, something contrary to God and at enmity with God.[18] It must be purged from the hearts of the believers.

Many of the believers have become saturated with the world, full of worldly "water." Consequently, they must be "dried out," and the worldly element purged from them. The heat of suffering during the tribulation will accomplish this.

When the children of Israel wandered in the wilderness they longed for the things of Egypt — for the leeks, onions, garlic, and the other Egyptian foodstuffs.[19] They had no taste for the heavenly manna. They called it light bread,[20] bread without taste. They desired to return to Egypt[21] for its strong, overpowering tastes.

So it will be with many believers during the endtime. Although the world will be taken away from them, they will still long for the things of the world — its luxuries, strong tasting "foods," ease of living, and amenities. It will take some time for that inward desire and longing for the world to come to an end. The tribulation will be a long drying-out period. On one hand the believers will be nourished to grow in the divine life, and on the other hand they will be dried out of the worldly water to be freed from the world and all the worldly tastes.

A Warning

And the woman fled into the wilderness, where she hath a place prepared of God, that there they may nourish her a thousand two hundred and threescore days. (Rev. 12:6)

Hidden within the verses that describe the woman fleeing into the wilderness is a very strong warning. There we are told that *they* will nourish the woman for 1260 days. Who are *they*? Who will nourish the woman?

These must be believers who are rich in the Word of God, who will provide spiritual nourishment to the rest of the believers at the end of the age. They must have spent a great deal of their lives studying and appropriating the Word, and ministering it to others. As a consequence they will be able to feed the believers during that time.

However, how is it that some who are rich in the Word, and have an abundance of the spiritual supply, would be left behind during those years? Why would they not be taken before the tribulation with the rest of the fully mature believers? It must be they will not have finished their course.

In spite of being rich in the Word, there will be some thing or things within them that they have not overcome, that has frustrated the growth of the divine life in them. Perhaps it is pride or some other serious inward fault. Perhaps they will see themselves as something special *because* they are rich in the Word. They may exalt themselves because of their ministry and success in feeding the saints God's word. They may be like Diotrephes[22] who was one who loved the preeminence. Spiritual pride is a very serious matter which results in extremely serious consequences. Whatever the case may be, something within will prevent them from overcoming fully and being prepared for the Lord's coming.

How great a shock it will be to those who, in spite of having an abundant supply of God's Word, are left behind to pass through that time of great suffering. May all those who minister God's Word take this warning to heart. It is not enough to minister God's Word. We must gain Christ in every part of our being in order that everything not of God — especially pride — be put to death on the cross of Christ in our experience.

Return

Come back! Return to Christ and Christ alone. Now is the time to drop all divisions, doctrines, rituals, positions, our self-esteem, high-mindedness, pride, and so many other religious and self-centered matters and return to Christ. Now is the time to come back to the wonderful, divine Person, and begin to experience the oneness of the triune God for which Christ prayed before His death.[23] Leave everything and come back to Christ!

References

[1] Jn. 16:20-21
[2] Rev. 12:4
[3] Rev. 12:10-11
[4] Rev. 12:14
[5] Rev. 12:12
[6] Rev. 12:15
[7] Rev. 12:16
[8] Rev. 7:3-8
[9] Matt. 10:16-23
[10] Rev. 18:4
[11] Rev. 19:11-21
[12] Rev. 3:10
[13] Jn. 3:5-6
[14] 1 Cor. 3:6-7; Col. 2:19 (Greek)
[15] Phil. 3:8
[16] Ps. 42:2; 63:1; 143:6; Rev. 22:17
[17] Rev. 14:15 (Greek)
[18] 1 Jn. 2:15; 5:19; Jm. 4:4
[19] Num. 11:5
[20] Num. 21:5
[21] Num. 14:3-4
[22] 3 Jn. 1:9
[23] Jn. 17:11, 21-23

CHAPTER 4

Hope

In previous books* in this series, the firstfruits have been described in detail. These are the first of God's people to fully mature. They will be taken from the earth before the last three and a half years of this age, before the time of trial coming upon the whole inhabited earth.[1] They will join the Lord Jesus in the heavens before the throne of God, where they will enjoy the divine Presence and sing praises to God in love as a satisfaction to the Father. How sweet that time will be! These will enter into the eternal state, their eternal dwelling in God. They will have finished their course just as the apostle Paul did.[2] They will be accounted worthy to escape all the trials and sufferings coming upon the earth and to stand before the Lord.[3]

However, very little detail has been provided about the majority of believers, those who will be left behind to pass through the endtime tribulation. It is important to realize that even if we are left behind to suffer the trials at the end of the age, there is still hope.

The situation, condition, and future of the believers should not be viewed in terms of black and white. As there will be degrees of discipline and punishment during the coming age,[4] so there will also be degrees of success. There are various shades between the white of the highest success and the black of the most abysmal failure. Consequently, even if one is left on earth during the endtime, all is not lost!†

---

*See *The Goal and Peak of Our Christian Experience* and *Firstfruits and Harvest*.

†However, don't use this hope as an excuse to love the world or the flesh today, expecting to mature later during the tribulation. That time will be unimaginably terrible. Do not choose it in return for some temporary pleasure or leisure today!

The Condition of the Believers

Among those who are left behind, there will be various cases and conditions. Some will have understood the need to be ready for the Lord's return, and yet still be unprepared. It may be that they did not give all to the Lord, that Christ was not pre-eminent to them. Perhaps they were attracted by the world and caught by it. Perhaps fame, mammon, or amusements distracted them from Christ and led to their failure in this age. They may not have heeded the apostle's word: "But far be it from me to glory, save in the cross of our Lord Jesus Christ, through which the world hath been crucified unto me, and I unto the world."[5] There are so many facets to the satanic world. It is easy to be led astray and entrapped by it.

Or, there may have been inward difficulties or obstacles. Perhaps some are unable or unwilling to face and overcome such inward problems. Due to fearfulness or unbelief they may turn from the path and fail.

Unknowing

Other believers may not know about the possibility of being left behind during the endtime. They may have wholeheartedly accepted the sugar-coated doctrines about the rapture of all the believers, not realizing the danger of this teaching. Or, they may simply have ignored the matters concerning the endtime. Whatever the case, these also may not be ready.

They may suffer from the same problems as those who did know and yet weren't ready. They may have some growth in the divine life and yet not have fully matured. Others may be like little children. They may have learned few, if any, of the life lessons that Christians must learn to grow and mature. These will have a very long way to go to finish their Christian course.

And then there are those who simply did not care. They gave themselves to other things, to the things of the world or to the flesh. These have been barely born and are spiritual babes. The endtime may be most difficult for them.

Growth

...holding fast the Head, from whom all the body, being supplied and joined together by the joints and bands, grows with the growth of God. (Col. 2:19*)

...as newborn babes, long for the spiritual milk which is without guile, that ye may grow thereby unto salvation... (1 Pet. 2:2)

...till we all attain unto the unity of the faith, and of the knowledge of the Son of God, unto a fullgrown man, unto the measure of the stature of the fulness of Christ... (Eph. 4:13)

The last three and a half years of this age will be a time to help all the Christians who have not yet matured spiritually to grow in Christ. The world will have been taken away from them. All the worldly enjoyments and endeavors will be gone. Sports, games, concerts, parties, restaurants, and every other worldly amusement will cease to exist. Worldly position, fame, and fortune will be over. Everything of the world will be destroyed. During those last years all the taste, love, and desire for the world within the believers will be dried up.[6] By the time of the Lord's return many Christians will have no more taste for the world, and desire Christ and Christ alone.

Those days will be a time of intense suffering — suffering from wounds and injuries, hunger and thirst, illness and disease, cold and exposure, and heat and exhaustion. Food, water, and medications will all be in short supply. For those who have lived a life in the flesh, their life of pleasure will become one of pain. Due to the outward situation and the endtime afflictions they will be forced from their flesh and toward Christ.[†] Through all this Christ will grow and be made strong in many.

While the believers on the earth during the tribulation will have missed the opportunity to be firstfruits and will be suffering through tremendous difficulties, this will not be a time for despair. There is still hope! The Lord will not abandon the believers.

---

*Greek

†Many times this is the reason afflictions beset us — to drive us to Christ.

Repentance

At that time the regret among God's people on earth will be intense. They will fear for what is coming upon the earth. They will be deeply troubled by being so totally unprepared for the endtime events. They will be greatly dismayed at having accepted the sugar-coated doctrines which teach that all the believers will be taken away before the great endtime troubles strike the earth. They will be angered and outraged at being duped by Satan and the world. They will be angry and upset at those Christian leaders who led them astray, and did not lead them to Christ and into the experience of Christ. They will be disgusted at the fleshy and frivolous divisions among Christians. In this state of inward upheaval, the Christians remaining on the earth will begin to reject doctrines, forms, rituals, and attempts at self-improvement through the keeping of the law. They will begin to see that all these are not only useless, but in large part the cause of their failure.

Among these dear Christians will be some who have the spiritual food supply and are able to nourish God's people. Though rich in the Word, for one reason or another they too will be left behind. As they minister the Word to the believers, many will be helped to drop all things for Christ, to inwardly let go of everything that they might gain Christ.[7] As they are fed, they will begin to grow. They will drop all the religious things that not only didn't help them, but actually frustrated their growth. These three and a half years will be a time of intensified feeding and maturation.

Encouragement

Behold, I come as a thief. Blessed is he that watcheth, and keepeth his garments, lest he walk naked, and they see his shame. (Rev. 16:15)

In the midst of all this trouble, suffering, dismay, and chaos the Lord speaks an encouraging word: "Blessed is he that watcheth, and keepeth his garments." These garments are the covering that results from the experience of Christ within. They are the change in character and person that results from abiding in Christ, looking to Him, and being near Him that is expressed in the living and the outward behavior of the believers. For those who do keep their garments, who experience Christ more and more and allow Him to be expressed through them, *a blessing awaits!* Although they may have been left behind during those last years, they may still be blessed.

The Wedding Feast

...Blessed are they that are bidden to the marriage supper of the Lamb. And he saith unto me, These are true words of God. (Rev. 19:9)

In Revelation 19 God reveals that wonderful blessing prepared for those who are properly "attired," who have experienced and gained Christ and through whom Christ is expressed: Blessed are those that are bidden to the marriage supper of the Lamb! These will be the guests during the thousand-year celebration of the Lamb's marriage.

However, they are not the bride, at least not yet. In eternity future, the bride of the Lamb is the New Jerusalem — the whole of all God's redeemed. That city is comprised of all the people of God from the time of Adam until the end of the millennium. She is the eternal wife of the Lamb. But during the millennium, the Lamb's bride is composed of those who have fully matured in Christ and become exactly like Him in every way.

Adam and Eve

And out of the ground Jehovah God formed every beast of the field, and every bird of the heavens; and brought them unto the man to see what he would call them: and whatsoever the man called every living creature, that was the name thereof. And the man gave names to all cattle, and to the birds of the heavens, and to every beast of the field; but for man there was not found a help meet for him. (Gen. 2:19-20)

Until he fell, the first man, Adam, was a type[8] of the coming Christ. Adam was looking for a counterpart, a companion suitable for him, one with whom he could share his life. God brought all the animals to Adam to be named. But among those Adam did not find one that was suitable to be his helper. This tells us that Adam was searching for a counterpart.

So God put Adam to sleep, took a bone from his side, and built that bone into a woman. When Adam saw the woman that God had made, he exclaimed, "This time it is bone of my bone and flesh of my flesh!"[9]

Since Adam was a type of Christ, this whole event in Adam's life was a picture of what was to come. On the cross Christ's side was opened, just as Adam's was, and out from that wound flowed blood and water.[10] The blood is, of course, for redemption. The water is a symbol of Christ as the divine life flowing out through His humanity, which was broken on the cross. This divine life is the very substance of Christ's bride, His counterpart.

However, in order to be the bride of Christ, the believers must match Christ in every way. As Adam rejected every animal brought to him and accepted only that which came forth from his side, so Christ's bride cannot contain anything natural, earthly, spotted, blemished, or anything other than Christ Himself. Christ Himself is the element, the substance of His bride.

Consequently, it is only those believers who are fully matured and in whom Christ is everything who comprise the bride. She includes all the firstfruits seen in Revelation 14 — every believer who has finished the course, attained the prize of God's high calling, reached the peak of the Christian experience, and become a perfect match for Christ.

However, there are many believers who have not yet finished their course. They may not require being cast into outer darkness[11] or lashed with stripes[12] as some believers will. They may be judged by Christ to have done well in their lives, even though they had not yet fully matured. The Lord will welcome these into His joy, into His wedding feast. These are the guests of the Lamb and His bride during the millennium.

How great this blessing will be! These dear guests will enjoy a thousand-year wedding feast with Christ and His bride. During that time Christ's presence in glory and the wonderful fellowship with all the believers there will be the exquisite portion of all in attendance. During that time all these will be brought to full maturity in Christ and enter the eternal state. They will become like Christ in every way just like the bride. Through this experience they will become part of the new Jerusalem, the eternal wife of the Lamb.

Pursue

...that I may know him, and the power of his resurrection, and the fellowship of his sufferings, becoming conformed unto his death... (Phil. 3:10)

And so there is still hope, even to those who are left behind on the earth for the last years of this age. If the believers pursue and gain Christ during the tribulation, then a blessing awaits them. We *must* not make the same mistake twice, in this age *and* again during the tribulation. No, pursue Christ!

As the word in Revelation 16 implies and warns, some *will* make that same mistake again. Some will not pursue Christ, even during the intense suffering at the end of the age. Sadly, some will stand naked and ashamed before Christ at His judgment seat,[13] having ignored Christ not only during their present lives but even during the tribulation.

However, many will take advantage of that time and suffering to know the Lord, gain Him, enjoy the power of His resurrection, and partake of the fellowship of His sufferings. In joy the Lord will welcome them into the millennial feast.

References

[1] Rev. 3:10
[2] 2 Tim. 4:7
[3] Lk. 21:36
[4] Lk. 12:47-48; Matt. 25:10, 30, e.g.
[5] Gal. 6:14
[6] Rev. 14:15 (Greek)
[7] Phil. 3:8
[8] Rom. 5:14
[9] Gen. 2:23
[10] Jn. 19:34
[11] Matt. 25:30
[12] Lk. 12:47-48
[13] 2 Cor. 5:10; Rom. 14:10

CHAPTER 5

A Final Word

In the preface to this book the rise of evil was mentioned. It may now be apparent what the evil one's plot is after reading the previous chapters.

God has a purpose[1] and a plan to accomplish that purpose. He desires to bring many sons into glory,[2] that they may stand before Him in love eternally.[3] In addition, they will inherit the earth[4] and reign over it.[5]

However, Satan also has his purpose and his plan. He desires to frustrate God's purpose, to keep God's sons from glory and from reigning on the earth. Initially, he attempts to stop them from being reborn. Then, after they contact God and are born of Him, Satan attempts to distract them from God and stunt their growth in the divine life by the world system he has created. By doing this he keeps himself in power over the earth.[6]

Move and Countermove

Satan has devised this world system to frustrate God's purpose and the growth of God's sons. He temporarily succeeds in some measure with many, but not all, of the believers. Some overcome all of Satan's distractions through the overcoming Christ who indwells them.[7]

For each of Satan's machinations God has a countermove. In particular, for His children who have been distracted by the satanic world God has a solution. On the one hand, God will destroy the world[8] Satan has used to distract the believers from Christ. On the other hand, God is preparing a place of refuge and isolation for the distracted believers, to which He will gather them by using the endtime persecution to force them to flee.

Of course Satan has a countermove to God's preparation of the wilderness. He is trying to destroy that place God is preparing.

If Satan could totally corrupt the United States, God would be forced to destroy it. Where then could God bring His children at the end of the age to nourish them and cause them to grow in Christ? If Satan can fully corrupt the United States this would totally disrupt God's move.

Satan Versus God

It is not a matter of left or right, liberal versus conservative. It is something far deeper, occurring in the invisible, spiritual realm behind the scenes. What is really happening is a battle of Satan versus God and of darkness versus light. Satan's intent is to so damage the United States by fully corrupting its cultural morality that this country becomes unusable to God. The godlessness of the atheists and the many other morally bankrupt and corrupt people in the United States that promote the dark, satanic agenda are all part of Satan's plot to thwart God's move for Christ's return.

We must understand that there are very many evil, dark people in the United States. These have aligned themselves with Satan and against God. They have become one with the darkness. Some do this unwittingly, having been blinded by Satan.[9] Others have full knowledge of what they are doing. In their great hatred of God they have chosen the way of the evil one, the way of immorality, perversion, abomination, deceit, hatred, division, and ultimate destruction. They desire to bring down the United States by corrupting and destroying it. They particularly hate God and God's people. They desire to do away with anything that in any way relates to God. They are acting according to the spirit of the Antichrist, who will hate all gods and all religions.[10]

Clarity

Knowing these things, we should be clear how to proceed. This knowledge will help us in our prayer, and guide us in our preparations. It will dispel any fog regarding our stance — what we stand for and what we stand against. It is not a matter of some political side. It is all about God's intent and purpose, and Satan's plot and attack.

As God's people standing for Him on the earth we must clearly see the battle in which we find ourselves. We must also know the enemy whom we are fighting. We must not be ignorant of Satan's devices.[11] We must pray much to keep the United States from the evil and destruction into which Satan is attempting to lead it. We must also pray for God's preparation of that place in the wilderness for His people during the tribulation.

Looking to the End

The last years of this age will be a time of enormous suffering. Many of those fleeing the persecution in the Far East and Europe will have been tortured. Others will suffer injuries of various kinds during the great cataclysms at the beginning of the tribulation. The whole earth will be turned upside down and the world as we know will be gone. Electricity, gas and oil supplies, foodstuffs, communications of all types, commerce, and so many other things common to our daily lives will be ended. Money will be useless. There will be shortages of all kinds — of food, water, medical supplies, shelter, and clothing. This dire situation will continue until the Lord returns. Everywhere those who remain alive, who have not been killed during the great upheaval, will be struggling to survive, especially during the time immediately following God's judgments.

What Must We Do?

Watch therefore: for ye know not on what day your Lord cometh. But know this, that if the master of the house had known in what watch the thief was coming, he would have watched, and would not have suffered his house to be broken through. Therefore be ye also ready; for in an hour that ye think not the Son of man cometh. (Matt. 24:42-44)

Watch therefore, for ye know not the day nor the hour. (Matt. 25:13)

But of that day or that hour knoweth no one, not even the angels in heaven, neither the Son, but the Father. Take ye heed, watch and pray: for ye know not when the time is. It is as when a man, sojourning in another country, having left his house, and given authority to his servants, to each one his work, commanded also the porter to watch. Watch therefore: for ye know not when the lord of the house cometh, whether at even, or at midnight, or at cockcrowing, or in the morning; lest coming suddenly he find you sleeping. And what I say unto you I say unto all, Watch. (Mk. 13:32-37)

But watch ye at every season, making supplication, that ye may prevail to escape all these things that shall come to pass, and to stand before the Son of man. (Lk. 21:36)

What shall we do? What *must* we do? Spiritually, we must watch. We must pray much, looking away from everything unto Jesus.[12] We must let go of all things and seek Christ,[13] desiring to gain Him just as the apostle Paul did.[14]

The Lord commanded us to watch and pray. He was quite strong. What He said to one He says to all: "Watch!" Indeed, He told us to watch and pray at every season that we might overcome and be accounted worthy to escape all these trials and stand before the Son of Man. By doing this we prepare ourselves for the Lord's return. It is those who have not overcome, who are not accounted worthy, who are left behind to pass through the tribulation. Let us therefore watch and pray continually.

Furthermore, we must watch because we don't know the hour of His coming. If we will not watch, He will come upon us as a thief, stealing away the precious believers who are ready for Him, yet leaving us behind. If we do watch and pray, then we might be accounted worthy to stand before Him in that day.

God's People

We must also pray for God's people. As a whole the believers are woefully unprepared for the Lord's return. Many will be left behind during the tribulation to grow in the divine life. Nevertheless, we must pray that they may be ready. And, as the Lord leads, we must pray for that place in the wilderness to be prepared for those left behind.

In all things we should pray according to the Lord's leading. This is the best way to prepare. We must pray not only for our own cooperation with the Lord, but for His leading in how to cooperate. He may show us some particular way in which He would use us during this time for that coming day.

Great Need

During the endtime the physical needs of God's people will be enormous. Food, both physical and spiritual, will be in short supply. There will be a need for both of these to be stored for that day. There will be a great need of shelter, particularly during the great upheaval. Even after that time, this need will continue because so much will have been destroyed by the earthquakes, enormous winds, and huge fires that will ensue from the great asteroid strikes. In addition, many will require medical treatment and healing. There will be much trauma of various kinds to God's people and to men in general. How great the need will be in that day for tender care, concern, and love.

Led by the Lord

As the Lord would lead, we should look forward to that day in prayer, not only for ourselves and our families, but also for God's people generally. Many will be left to pass through that trial. They will be unprepared and vulnerable. How many of the ones who remain behind will have enormous needs. They also must be in our hearts, in our prayers, and in our considerations.

It is not yet the endtime, nor is it the time to begin making physical preparations. We must wait until that day comes when it is time to act. As we see the day of the Lord's return nearing and the Antichrist's ten-nation empire beginning to form, that may be the time for us to take appropriate steps in preparation.

However, now is the time to prepare spiritually. We must prepare by watching, praying, and seeking the Lord. In our preparation we are saving our own souls.

References

[1] Eph. 3:11
[2] Heb. 2:10
[3] Eph. 1:4
[4] Matt. 5:5
[5] Rev. 20:4
[6] Eph. 2:2
[7] Jn. 16:33; 1 Jn. 4:4
[8] Rev. 6:12-17; 8:1-12
[9] 2 Cor. 4:4
[10] Dan. 11:36-37; Rev. 17:16-17
[11] 2 Cor. 2:11
[12] Heb. 12:2
[13] Phil. 3:10-12
[14] Phil. 3:8

BIBLIOGRAPHY

Cozza, Paul. *The Coming End of the Age*. A Place in the Wilderness, 2016

Vincent, Marvin R. *Word Studies in the New Testament*. Grand Rapids:Wm. B. Eerdmans Publishing Co., 1977

www.ingramcontent.com/pod-product-compliance
Lightning Source LLC
Chambersburg PA
CBHW061225070526
44584CB00029B/3988